NO GOOD THINGS DWELL IN THE FLESH

Christina Masciotti

BROADWAY PLAY PUBLISHING INC
New York
www.broadwayplaypublishing.com
info@broadwayplaypublishing.com

Cover photo: Maria Baranova

First edition: December 2023
I S B N: 979-8-88856-002-0

Book design: Marie Donovan
Page make-up: Adobe InDesign
Typeface: Palatino

NO GOOD THINGS DWELL IN THE FLESH was first produced at the Jeffrey and Paula Gural Theatre at A.R.T./New York Theatres opening on 10 September 2023. The cast and creative contributors were:

AGATA .... Kelley Overbey
JANICE..Carmen Zilles
VLAD.. T Ryder Smith
CUSTOMERS/POLICE......Megan Lomax & Jeffrey Brabant

Director...Rory McGregor
Set .... Brendan Gonzales Boston
Costumes.. Johanna Pan
Lighting.. Stacey Derosier
Sound ....Brian Hickey

CHARACTERS & SETTING

AGATA, *Russian master tailor, 64, female*

JANICE, *her apprentice, 30, female*

VLAD, *her former suitor, 65, male*

CUSTOMERS ONE-EIGHT/POLICE. *the full range, 20-70, male/female*

Casting Note: the CUSTOMERS/POLICE can be split between two actors with the odd-numbered CUSTOMERS/POLICEWOMAN played by a female actor and the even-numbered CUSTOMERS/POLICEMAN played by a male actor.

Time: 2019

A tailor shop in Queens

Scene 1

(A cozy tailor shop in Queens. About ten feet up each wall, a motley assortment of garments appears to levitate. Sober interview suits, flashy zebra prints, ragged denim, and puffs of prom tulle seethe with infectious life.)

(A fitting room curtain anchors one side of the shop, with a storefront glass door on the other.)

(AGATA enters and pauses at her indestructible tank of a machine, reassured. She dons a work vest and glasses, reinvigorated by her no-frills uniform of practical efficiency. But just as she's about to dive into work, a spectral tentacle of smoke creeps into the frame of her storefront window.)

(Inexplicably, another wisp of smoke unfurls inside the shop, right before her eyes. She turns toward the glass door, resolute.)

AGATA: I don't believe too deeply Charles Darwin. One thing I like about him: strongest one survive. If you stupid enough to smoke, then be dead.

(JANICE enters with a surge of brightness, energy, and effervescence.)

JANICE: The sky is so strange.

AGATA: Who?

JANICE: No, the sky. Half blue. Half gray.

AGATA: Oh, I thought you said *this guy.*

JANICE: *(Looking out the window)* I wish he wouldn't smoke right outside his shop. It comes in here.

AGATA: How did you do with the sleeves?

JANICE: Oh, I didn't have time. Sorry.

AGATA: I thought you had Saturday nights off.

JANICE: I do. I went on a date last night.

(Pause)

AGATA: It doesn't matter what you see I do with my hands, if your hands don't practice. You won't know where to keep your finger. How to regulate distance. Like driving car. Everyone knows: keep wheel straight. Try it the first time, it won't be so straight. You have to practice until you have feelings in wheel. In pedal when you press. You need this feelings.

JANICE: I know. I was about to start doing the sleeves, but then I got a message on my profile, and this guy was actually asking me out. And it just hit me: If I stay home tonight, I'm literally choosing to be a spinster. So I had to go out. Even though I totally regret it and it was a complete waste of time.

AGATA: Another one you didn't like.

JANICE: He said, "cool cool" after everything I said. You know? I don't think I wanna go out with someone who says "cool cool."

AGATA: Does he have good job?

JANICE: He's a forensic linguist.

AGATA: Forensic?

JANICE: Yeah, what's that mean, right? The *language* of crime scenes? How fascinating. But no. He's just a translator in court. From France. Who I could tell wasn't wearing deodorant. Man. He seemed so perfect in the chat. Like the kind of guy I'd actually want to date.

AGATA: What is that?

JANICE: Shy. American. Funny. Like Hugh Grant.

AGATA: That guy? He's British asshole like Winston Churchill.

JANICE: I swear the only thing he had going for him was his profile pic. It was him, casual at the stove, stirring spaghetti sauce. Not even looking at the camera. I thought great, he's not too into himself. But I checked it this morning and he changed it to a smoldering close up! Can you believe that? I can't cringe any harder. I'm throwing my back out cringing.

AGATA: Is he tall?

JANICE: Like six feet.

AGATA: Short men have more ambition. As taller, you see like sheep. They don't know anything unless wife here, tells them what to do. And they never have ten dollars in pocket. Leave clothes here so long they covered in dust. I have two things I already gave away from someone I called a thousand times.

JANICE: I'm okay with tall.

AGATA: All great leaders were shorter men. As taller men are, more stupid. Certain amount proud of themself. For *nothing*.

JANICE: I deleted my profile, so he can't contact me again. (*Pause*) I can't believe I thought it meant something when the card I pulled from the CBT deck I use was "Expect the Best." Right before the date. I was like, it's true. Not *everything* can possibly be a disaster. Wrong.

AGATA: If you want to meet people, why don't you go to the gym? Whole rhythm of people, kind of inspiring. Men so good looking. Successful. I met a couple people interesting. A yoga trainer. Her eyes so deep, so something catching. She told me: "You look like my mom exactly." Her mom from Russia like me.

JANICE: I thought you were from Latvia.

AGATA: I lived in Latvia, but I was citizen of Soviet Union. When Russia broken, I lost citizenship. That why I left. *(Focusing on dress)* This dress is so complicated. Watch what I do. This strip is a imitation of belt.

(JANICE *scrolls through her phone.*)

AGATA: Janice, are you watching?

JANICE: *(Without looking up)* Yeah.

AGATA: *(Running the machine)* This tension of thread I change for seam to look better. Stitch has length number four. *(About the new stitches)* See, I can pull and gather. In general, loose tension you can do more things. *(Pause)* Did you see how much space I left between the belt and dress?

JANICE: *(To her phone)* Mm-hmm.

AGATA: This belt. Many places needs to be attached. Eight places. *(Pause)* Janice, if you don't watch me—

JANICE: *(Looking up)* I'm watching!

AGATA: Janice, listen. I don't wanna force you.

JANICE: I'm sorry, I can't concentrate right now.

(AGATA *throws a garment in front of her.*)

AGATA: If can't concentrate, work. I have eight double piping belt loops for you to finish. Very complicated. Fold them, stitch one time, fold it, flip it, stitch the triangle. Fabric is thick, can't mark it. A brushed wool, very much visible when you make mistake.

JANICE: I'm too jittery, I can't.

AGATA: Start working, stop shaking. Think like zippers. You came every week my class in zippers. Many drop and don't come back. Too complicated. Every millimeter count when you install zipper. You didn't give up. When you work, you work very well. That why I gave you class for free. Instead of pay me, ask you come here and help me.

JANICE: I didn't know that. I thought you were desperate for help.

AGATA: No, I care about what I do. If bad poet, rather swipe streets, at least see result of job. Nothing there, I tell you to stop plain. I can see what you do. Past few months, you do lovely job.

JANICE: When I was little I made dresses for toys. I couldn't sew. I glued. You know my ancestors are from Brazil. Someone told me all my previous people are tailors. It's in my blood.

AGATA: That beautiful. You and I are from the same cloth. You need to develop this talent.

JANICE: Yeah. Before now, the only time I ever really did was as a Home Health Aide. If that counts.

AGATA: You was a Home Health Aide?

JANICE: Only for a couple years. It was a miserable job. I made nine twenty-five an hour. But I kept showing up because it was better than being alone.

AGATA: And seamstressing was part of that job?

JANICE: Not officially. But my last client kind of took me under her wing. I'd sit with her, knitting. She'd correct me when I messed up the count. She was the only person who treated me well. I guess she liked me.

AGATA: You were kind of good match.

JANICE: One day, she showed me a wool coat she couldn't wear. It was too long. She was gonna give it to me. It was so beautiful, I couldn't accept it. I offered to shorten it for her. She didn't believe I could. (Pause) It was an old-fashioned coat that flared out like a dress. A little tattered where she stepped on it. It was a dark, navy color. I measured the thing every five or six inches and marked with a chalk she had. The pins she had were terrible. None of them were sharp. *(Pause)* But it came out perfect. She put it on and looked so good, she said, "When it's my time to fly to the rainbow, this what I wanna be wearing."

(Pause)

AGATA: Tailor are special people. You know it's dying profession. Your teacher says same.

JANICE: Yeah, he agrees with you.

AGATA: Everybody knows dying profession. It's dying because it's hard way to learn and you have to be creative. People doesn't wanna learn. It's time taking. Again, again until perfection. You never see young people working in alterations. You can be lawyer or doctor in ten years. Can't be alterations in ten years. Now click on internet, make a lot of money. With this you can't just click, you have to work a hundred years. I prefer this but. Last week, I was stitching so many things, I fell asleep on my couch. Tomorrow will be third, I have to do jacket, two things will go home with me. At home I don't have that spare of a moment. I can't continue like this. All of a suddenly, I realized in twelve years I had one vacation. I'm sixty-four. Life will be over soon. I need a vacation.

JANICE: I could cover for you for a couple weeks.

AGATA: Yes. Maybe longer.

JANICE: Yeah, sure.

AGATA: Years maybe.

JANICE: What do you mean?

(Pause)

AGATA: You could take over the whole thing.

JANICE: Your tailor shop?

AGATA: Think about. You have business degree.

JANICE: Which I've been putting to great use bartending. I know exactly how much I'm ripping people off with each pour. Microbrew crap, easily four hundred percent and no one blinks an eye.

AGATA: Not everyone thinks like businesswoman, like you. You have that background. Soon you have your FIT degree. What more you need to run this shop?

JANICE: I think you're underestimating the fact that you're like a genius with thread.

AGATA: This from practice. That all. I taught myself. Skill build from time spend practicing. Before I was civil engineer. I thought I could find job somewhere as engineer with whole benefits. But my paper didn't work here. So step by step, by myself, I make plan, I follow it. This what I do with belt, I think I met it on YouTube. I just in love with it. *(Pause)* That what you have to do. Read about sewing couture. I have every issue Thread magazine, I will give you. I did own research on how to knit. Put parts together when finish. When to increase stitches when to decrease. Smaller, bigger, bigger, bigger have a little curves. I can calculate without any computer a single simple formula. Soon you see person as form. That form cover person. How best cover person. *(Pause)* In museums, too. Go very close to big pieces fabric embroidery. See what kind of stitches. Some guards paranoid. But those little stitches so precious. Every machine has special way to stitch. Hand stitches different every tailor. The tailor, sitting. Stick of candle all night. So big respect for tailors. Independent, alone. Only politics: to make as best as possible. This is my politics.

JANICE: Agata, I'm honored, but I could never afford to buy your business.

AGATA: Don't pay me. Take it over. That how you pay me.

JANICE: I'm not just gonna take it from you.

AGATA: There's nothing to buy. There's no name on it. Just "Tailor Shop." It's not Giorgio Armani. I chose the name "Tailor Shop" why? Because whatever do name business, first important word. People start to check online. Who cares about my name? They're looking for tailors. Tailor in Astoria. Google it. It pops.

JANICE: Agata, this is America. You can't just give away your business. You have to dupe someone into paying ten times its valuation.

AGATA: If you trick people, karma will hit you back. I don't do.

JANICE: But you always say, "If you give something for free, people will never appreciate." That's humanity. You have to fight for it.

AGATA: Janice, it look like my baby here. I don't like to abandon my baby. I take it to be same as I am. I want things will continue. Continuing life. People deserve to have professional do things. I've been looking for someone since I started business. Yelp told me I must find. Called: "Advertise with us. Five star business. Bad reviews, don't worry we'll fix it." I say, "I have plenty people come here. If more, I can't sew so much." He say, "Think like good businesswoman. Find assistant." I had so many people try. Nobody able to do things - something like quality. Need to have your inside willing to do it. Something like passion, something attracting you in it. Nobody had that.

JANICE: Agata, I'm really flattered, but—

AGATA: Yelp company hundred percent corrupted place. I didn't advertise, so they put bad review on. Then they send bad customers. They're like money extortion. One time mine so low, only 3 stars, full of bad reviews just to break me. It's not the truth what they write. Like the KGB collecting all this information: my moral side not good; I speak too open; my ideology not good enough to travel abroad, introduce self to country as Soviet Union because I watch German magazines and take style from the enemy.

JANICE: Don't worry about Yelp. Nobody reads Yelp.

AGATA: I was planning to take a lawyer. He said do nothing. Ignore them. Whoever wouldn't come, read who know what, who cares? Who is appreciate quality work, they come back. Whoever doesn't, I let them out. God bless them. Lawyer is right. I always have customers. If no one's here, people lose something. It's so need for people. It's so important. If you able to do it, it's so big pleasure. Just think about. Weigh the prons and cons.

(ONE enters.)

JANICE: *(To* ONE*)* Hi. We'll be right with you.

AGATA: *(To* JANICE*)* Look, I have this nice thread here. You finish this belt. Keep room. When wear, dress expand on body:One-sixteenth inches help belt look better.

JANICE: Okay.

AGATA: *(To* ONE*)* What I can do for you?

ONE: I have a skirt I need fitted.

AGATA: *(Gruffly, focused on her machine)* Try. We'll see what I can do.

(Pause. ONE *doesn't understand.)*

JANICE: You can try it on in the fitting area right over there. Come out when you're ready.

ONE: Thanks.

(ONE *steps behind a curtain.* AGATA *observes* JANICE.)

AGATA: You see? On top of all this, you know how to interact with people. You know what to say. You're a person type of person. You see everything pinky color. No bad words. Everything pinky for you. Pinky beautiful. Need to be diplomat like you. I'm different culture. Very tough. In this country, people would sue me completely. I don't want to upset anybody. I say things because I have to. Otherwhy, I go home bite nails and take antidepressant.

(ONE *emerges in a drop-waist skirt.*)

AGATA: Can you step over here? Face to the mirror.

(ONE *does so.*)

AGATA: Which part you want me to alter?

ONE: It feels really big here.

AGATA: That type of skirt, they're always troublemakers. They call it yoke. A miniskirt yoke. Should have darts here. Should be on hips not higher. If I change this, it will never stay on waist. It will go up to boobs. Keep on hips, or don't do it.

ONE: Can't you add elastic?

AGATA: No, it won't look nice.

ONE: It'll look better than cinching it with safety pins.

AGATA: Look I'm a professional tailor, if piece doesn't come out nice, I don't do it. If you wanna do like that, go to a dry cleaner. Maybe they know some secret I don't know. Or it should be done professional, or I won't do. I'm sorry, I can't just destroy things.

(ONE *goes back to the fitting area.* AGATA *and* JANICE *are silent. One emerges, livid.*)

JANICE: Sorry, we couldn't be more help!

(ONE *exits.*)

JANICE: Whoa. She had big plans for that skirt and she didn't care what rhyme or reason.

AGATA: When I worked at Bloomingdale's, customer asked me to do a skirt like that and I did it. Lady came back, she don't like skirt. My manager asked, "Why'd you do that?" She forced me to. "No one can force you." If you're professional, and know not good looking, don't do. Here, if I see something will not be good looking, I just don't take it. It's like committing crime. Crime of fashion.

Scene 2

(JANICE *is alone.* VLAD *enters through the glass door, his clothes accented by a Rolex and flip flops.*)

VLAD: Where is Agata?

(JANICE *looks up from a notebook.*)

JANICE: She stepped out. Can I help you?

(Pause)

VLAD: Who are you?

JANICE: Hi. I'm Janice.

(VLAD *stares at* JANICE.*)

JANICE: *(Extending a hand)* Nice to meet you!

VLAD: Why?

JANICE: *(Dropping her hand)* Sorry if that came out over-friendly. I get a little loud when I'm nervous. *(Closing her notebook)* Oh my god. *(Flipping it back open)* I bought this notebook at a thrift store and I just found this message on the last page: "Blondie, it's been so long since I saw you sleeping peacefully that I didn't want to awake you. Be careful out there and I'll see you at the farm.

Love, Bill." *(Amused)* What the hell? Are they like spies or something?

(VLAD *remains stone-faced.*)

VLAD: You know how to recognize who's spy? *(Pause)* They're simple, normal people. Can't tell by looking. Pay attention to feeling. Look them straight to face. If you feel everything on the inside crumbling down, that's a spy.

(Pause)

JANICE: I'm sorry. I didn't catch your name.

VLAD: All the above.

JANICE: Okay. Who would you like me to say stopped by?

VLAD: I'll wait.

(VLAD *seats himself. Awkward moments of silence.* JANICE *becomes increasingly uncomfortable with the way he studies her. He shifts to studying the lock on the door. Finally,* AGATA *enters. She plays it cool.*)

AGATA: You found me.

(AGATA *walks past* VLAD *and situates herself behind her machine.*)

VLAD: That's how you greet me?

AGATA: I didn't invite you.

(VLAD *gets up.*)

VLAD: Can I hug you?

AGATA: No, I'm sitting here doing business. If you come and try to hug me, I'm gonna hit you with this ruler.

VLAD: If you hit me, I'll hit you back. *(Pause)* You know how long it takes to knock out a woman? Thirty seconds. I know because I did it.

AGATA: Good. You can leave now and go find a woman to knock down.

VLAD: I have something I need fixed. Can I show you? *(He unfurls a pair of white Fruit of the Loom briefs.)* What I have in mind, not a simple thing. I need you to put on underwear, a little pocket with zipper, tight.

AGATA: You bring me your underwear.

VLAD: I need to smuggle money through Custom. Two pockets. When I go to Romania have to put declaration. Custom read it and rob you.

AGATA: I'm not able to do that type of job.

VLAD: *(Poking his finger through)* But look, this one also has a little tear here.

AGATA: I can't alter this.

VLAD: If you don't take care, it's gonna get worse.

AGATA: Stop creating all this situation.

VLAD: Janice, can you help me?

(VLAD dangles the underwear in front of JANICE's face.)

AGATA: Vlad, my patience broken. *(She grabs the underwear and hurls them to the floor.)*

VLAD: Why you turn everything against me?

AGATA: I'm on a schedule here. You think you're gonna come and spoil while I work? That why I never gave you address. I don't want you to come and reach me. Goodbye, please.

(VLAD collects his underwear.)

VLAD: Agata, let me ask you a question. *(Pause)* Why do you have a single lock on the door? You should have a second one. This, you could open even without a key. Put some dead locks. *(He exits.)*

JANICE: Um. Who the hell was that?

AGATA: Nobody. How did you do with that belt?

JANICE: I spent so much time. It would probably take you twenty minutes.

AGATA: Yes, maybe less. (*Examining the belt*) It's pinching here.

JANICE: I re-did it twice.

AGATA: It's okay. I'll fix.

(AGATA *rips out* JANICE's *stitches.*)

JANICE: You're really not gonna tell me what that guy was doing here?

AGATA: I have no idea.

JANICE: How do you know him?

AGATA: I met him at Bloomingdale's. He did fitting. We start to speak. He was happy, wants to do again. Asked what day I'll be working, introduce self, gave business card. He is intelligent man, not bad looking. Twelve years ago, I look younger. We met. He is Romanian from Venezuela. Knew no one here in US. He understand. Experience emigrate like newborn. Old, know nothing. Even don't know what time you need to laugh. Go back, people don't understand you. Say hello, no conversation. He was compassion. I understand his childhood experience in Venezuela. Couldn't speak. Children laugh to him. We became friends, lovers.

JANICE: Oh. *Damn.*

AGATA: Every man in my life, I left. I had no good relationship with a man ever in my life.

JANICE: What about your husband?

AGATA: I left my husband twice. That time. Society created: became that age you have to have husband or you're loser. I was happy to have that. I was thinking: good have family. Sit around table. Holidays.

Everything a dream. But in very short time, not what you planning to do. Almost never work.

Something else, else, else. Partner must be strong like you. He wasn't. He say: yes, yes, yes. And he was heavy drinker. He could not stop. I thought when we met, he told me about childhood. Good person for me. I was looking for the same. We didn't live together. Then all of a suddenly, married and live, and he was drunk. So I divorce my husband.

JANICE: Twice?

AGATA: Well, my daughter sees someone tall, blond hair, and calls, "Papa." I was embarrassed - so I thought let's do another shot.

JANICE: How old were you when you got married the second time?

AGATA: Thirty.

JANICE: Oh my god, I haven't even been married once yet!

AGATA: This is good thing, Janice.

JANICE: Is it? *(Pause)* I can't dry off in the shower without hitting my elbows. *(Demonstrating)* Ow. Ow. Ow. Ow. Ow. *(Pause)* The mattress on my bed is so hard it's like sleeping on a curb. I roll off and wake up on the floor. In my mom's laundry room. With a broken clothes dryer. It spins, but there's no heat. That's my life.

AGATA: Young woman sometimes have fear. Unsecurity. Think, need man to fulfill life. This from prehistorical times. Can't go for hunt protection. Women very much depend on men. And men took advantage. Eat like pigs. Big fists. I'll submit you. I'll have sex when I need it. I'll beat you up when I need it. This rules: certain age, husband, family; very old fashioned way. Look at the Romans. How they were killing their girlfriends with snakes. I mean this is grotesque. They do this because they're afraid of women. Why? Because we are smartest one. Women can think two parts of brain. Men only one.

JANICE: What, like men only want sex?

AGATA: No, men brain work just one side of the brain. It doesn't function both side. Woman left baby in bed. Baby crying. Husband watching TV. "Don't you hear baby crying?" He wasn't able to hear. I can talk to you, I sew, and if I had a baby, I'd listen to the baby. Three places, four places immediately.

JANICE: Oh, like multi-tasking.

AGATA: Men can't do. Instead men, I prefer spend time with my cat. Very independent, too. Don't want to be too much held. I respect that. Special sense of navigation like birds. Special sense of when owner come home. I know he likes me to come with this short expression: I come home, he purrs. He like water. Water dropping. Half his body covered little pills. He wants to grab this water shower, bites the water drops. Jump in Frigidaire. Just jump from floor to freezer because you can't expect. I let him sit. Try to pull out, he bites you. He find small boxes special. Warm cozy. Like a cave. Feel protected small space. The cat I admire. I am compassion to men, but I try to stay away.

Scene 3

(AGATA *sits at her desk.* VLAD *enters through the glass door with pants draped over his arm like a waiter.*)

VLAD: How much to alter pants?

AGATA: Fifteen dollars.

VLAD: Other guy said seven.

AGATA: You should go straight to him then.

VLAD: No, I prefer you.

AGATA: If you want me to alter pants, I will. Change it, please.

(VLAD *registers a moment of surprise and goes to the fitting area. He emerges, looking bizarre in ill-fitting pants from another time and continent.*)

AGATA: Face to the mirror.

(VLAD *turns.*)

AGATA: What type alterations?

(VLAD *stares at himself silently.*)

AGATA: Shorten? Take in?

VLAD: I don't know. I don't have stand-up mirror at home.

AGATA: Okay, look.

(VLAD *looks at* AGATA *in the mirror.*)

VLAD: The first time I came, you didn't give me any smile.

AGATA: You didn't come in theater comedy club. You came to tailor. I don't give fake smile.

VLAD: You used to smile right and left.

AGATA: Listen, for my opinion, I don't need you here. You need something from tailor, tell me, otherwhy, you go.

(*Pause*)

VLAD: Are the pants too short?

AGATA: They're short because they're slim on the bottom.

VLAD: I wanted them lower. When I sit, my ankle shows.

AGATA: The opening is not wide, so it won't fall down, not matter what.

VLAD: So you think this is good length?

AGATA: I think what you think.

VLAD: I must have weird body shape. Nothing fits.

AGATA: They fit. It's just the style.

VLAD: I don't want it baggy down there, but if it could be kind of full break that would be good.

AGATA: That not possible. Too narrow opening.

VLAD: *(Noticing fraying belt loops)* They put so much string here and still it comes off.

AGATA: Well, nothing forever. With time, it'll come off.

VLAD: What about the waist? Should I take it out?

AGATA: You feel tight?

VLAD: When I tried at the store, it felt tight. Now it doesn't.

AGATA: Maybe you didn't eat today.

VLAD: Do they shrink when you get dry cleaned?

AGATA: A little. If you let out half inch, it won't affect length.

VLAD: You think the length's okay?

AGATA: Okay for what?

VLAD: *(Frustrated)* You need someone here to give fashion tip!

AGATA: I would never do this. Between fashion tips and sewing, two different departments. You have to go with what you like. You don't know if you want it short, long, tight, or loose, I can't help you.

VLAD: Maybe they actual feel loose. How do you know if they should be taken in?

(AGATA sticks her hand down the back of his pants.)

AGATA: Should be two fingers. Fits my whole hand. Yes, can be taken two inches. I'll pin it.

(AGATA *starts to pin the back of his pants.* VLAD *revels in her attention.*)

VLAD: You have such nice perfume.

AGATA: You know I do sometimes wear for good mood. I regret I wore some today.

VLAD: I regret I came with only one pair of pants. Your touch is so pleasant. I missed you, Agata.

(VLAD *reaches around to grab* AGATA*'s forearm. She takes a step back.*)

AGATA: Take your pants. Get out.

(VLAD *grabs the fitting room curtain and tries to obscure* AGATA *from the front window.*)

(*As he pulls at her, she hurls her knee to his groin. He keels over.*)

AGATA: Go.

(VLAD *hobbles toward the door.* JANICE *enters as he stumbles out.*)

JANICE: (*To* AGATA) Oh my god, are you okay?

AGATA: I'm fine.

JANICE: Should I call the police?

AGATA: No.

JANICE: What did he do?

AGATA: You saw what I did. And I'm only second level weight, how it called, lifting. I have to pass ten levels more to be excellent.

JANICE: This is serious. We have to do something.

AGATA: If he was stranger, I am agree with you. But I know him. He's nothing to worry about. We were lovers, three, four years on and off. Why was off? In between in psychiatric institution. Before he became completely cuckoo with head, he was director. Head of bridges. Interested in languages. He knew a few. Graduated college well.

JANICE: That's wonderful he did so well in college and everything, but he just tried to assault you.

AGATA: I'm fine.

JANICE: That doesn't make it okay. We're sitting here in like a little cage.

AGATA: He's not some kind of mafia organizer. He's just thirty years on Prozac, and the Prozac stopped to work. That all. He start to feel very bad. We walk down the street, he say, "How come I can't be like those people?" Brainless, walking with children. "Why can't I be like them? I'll never be happy." He was planning to have family. Never family. Women wanted. He said, "I couldn't. Something keep me out of it." Blaming everybody. Parents not sensitive to his needs. Father had antique store. Not poor. He had plenty, plenty, plenty money. And *still* psychopath. Once I saw on table a book. "How to be Around Psychopaths." Wasn't novel. Instructions how to act. I asked him, "Why you read this?" He says, "All my family are psychopaths." I thought: not all your family. *You.* Whatever movie he watch from 1948 to 1950, man kill wife. I hate that movie. Put her in fireplace and burn there. He says, "This is the most interesting movie, see what they do?"

JANICE: I think we should close down the shop for the day.

AGATA: We can't, I have so many people picking up today.

JANICE: Then at least for a few hours so we can file a police report.

AGATA: Where's my needle? Where's my chalk?

JANICE: Agata, this is grounds for a restraining order. I can find out what precinct we're in. *(Searching on her phone)* We can go together—

AGATA: No, thank you.

JANICE: Why not?

AGATA: The police are useless. When I came here with my daughter, I ordered some furniture from Jennifer Convertible. We had nothing. Blanket for bed, second blanket was a pillow. Came home, I was robbed. I called police, they was vegetable lasagna. Nothing from them. Didn't even come.

JANICE: Do you honestly feel safe here?

AGATA: Yes.

JANICE: I don't. What if he comes back?

AGATA: Let him. I'm curious to see what he'll do next.

JANICE: For real?

AGATA: My major reason to be involved with him was I like to analyze. Tell the truth, I knew he was psychopath in my head. But I like to think. How far he can push? Curiosity of relationship with crazy man, driving me.

JANICE: Be careful, Agata, curiosity kills the cats.

AGATA: It won't kill me. I'm fine. I always had state of mind, think deeply. I read horoscope. Horoscope was prohibited. When country become open, I read Chinese horoscope, forty years old. I thought, okay, I'm not crazy. I'm Virgo.

JANICE: So we're not going to the police?

AGATA: No.

JANICE: Can I tell my boyfriend then?

AGATA: What boyfriend?

JANICE: Eddie. I didn't tell you about him?

AGATA: You tell me about new boyfriend every day.

JANICE: No, this is different.

AGATA: Mmm.

JANICE: I mean it. He always texts me back. Like immediately. So yeah, there's no question. He's really my boyfriend. And, he's a Marine. A very serious death stare is his resting face. All he has to say is, "Is there a problem?" And Vlad will never show up here again.

AGATA: You found him on the computer?

JANICE: No. He was like the most popular, most beautiful boy in my high school. His best friend was Statutory Cory, so I kept my distance. But he liked a photo I posted last month and he commented that he always had a secret crush on me. Can you believe that?

AGATA: What?

JANICE: How bold he is.

AGATA: Bold?

JANICE: To reveal his feelings in a public forum like that? Guys don't do that.

AGATA: I don't know if I call that on the computer bold.

JANICE: I mean he didn't care what anyone else would think. He wasn't afraid of rejection. That's impressive for a guy.

AGATA: No. This what I call bold. (*Pause*) My father was in war time. In concentration camp two and a half years. War end. Sent to other prison. Doing coal underground. Not honor prisoner of war. That mean you loser, you have to kill self. My father didn't even have weapon. Gave him a shovel to dig holes to hide in. Someone comes to you, you can't kill self with a shovel. (*Pause*) Big street. Father's name Paul. Pavel, other language. Rule: morning time go certain places take vegetables. March. Whoever fall, nobody give hands to get up. If

do, they kill man on ground, then you. They marching.
One man collapse. He called father's name. *(Pause)*
Father gave him hand. *(Pause)* That what I call bold.

JANICE: Okay. But I'm talking about this day and age.

AGATA: This day and age maybe I would do, too. If they
would kill you, just one time they kill you, that all.
Maybe less suffering.

JANICE: So can I tell him?

AGATA: It's your business what you tell him. Did you
finish the shirt I gave you?

JANICE: Yes.

AGATA: Can I see?

(JANICE presents the shirt. AGATA tests the buttons.)

JANICE: Did I mess it up?

AGATA: No, you did very nice work.

(JANICE basks in the compliment.)

AGATA: Difficult to hem way how it was designed. That
type of hem comes in twice a year. Maybe once. But for
that woman's bust it's a little tight. It might be too big
pressure on button. Should be like that, hanging a little.

JANICE: I just did the stitches like you showed me on the
other blouse. I forgot who brought it in.

AGATA: Yes, this is standard stitches. But every woman
has specific her needs. Exactly show off body nice. I
adjust for her.

JANICE: No, I can loosen the buttons. You have too much
to do.

Scene 4:
Parade of Customers

(AGATA *can't decide what to do first: she may shift from swiping an iron to hemming a cuff to patching a hole. She takes a vinyl tape measure and snaps it taut, but it somehow becomes more elastic, stretching into a long, wavy strip of bubble gum, misshapen and useless.*)

(*Suddenly, an endless stream of* CUSTOMERS *emerges like a fever dream. They march with self- conscious tics of discomfort, pulling at their sleeves and waists, trying to fix what's wrong.* TWO *gets* AGATA*'s attention.*)

TWO: Hey.

AGATA: Where you been all this time?

TWO: Busy man.

AGATA: (*Handing him a bag*) You go home to try. If you something unhappy, come back.

TWO: (*Handing her money*) I still need to pay.

AGATA: Oh you gave me a tip, right? Thank you.

TWO: There's one ATM that gives tens instead of twenties. I always go there.

AGATA: Ten is better than twenty?

TWO: I like them. I also brought this. (*He models a jacket.*)

AGATA: Sleeves a little long. You don't see yourself unfortunately, but over here doesn't look nice. Collar stands behind you. Collar should be hugging back. You can move buttons to make slimmer.

TWO: Do you have a tissue? I'm sweating.

AGATA: I'll give you right now. So let me move buttons and shorten sleeves. Can you relax please? Supposed to be short like that and down. Should be shirt half inch shorter.

TWO: What about the pants?

AGATA: When pleats on front, I do not recommend that job, tapering. Narrower you'll be looking like pear upside down. When you buy things, pay attention. It's old suit. I would never buy it.

(TWO *exits.* THREE *enters.*)

THREE: I need a big favor.

AGATA: I hope you're not asking me to do quickly because I can't.

THREE: But I just need this hole repaired for tonight.

AGATA: Why don't you take it and stitch it, see how long it takes.

(THREE *exits.* FOUR *enters.*)

FOUR: My pants are too wide. I need a modern fit.

AGATA: Do you have the right shoes?

FOUR: Pardon?

AGATA: Dress pants must have dress shoes.

FOUR: I'm not gonna be doing much more than typing in these pants.

AGATA: Take shoes and come back.

(FIVE *enters.*)

AGATA: You found some cute coat.

FIVE: It's Club Monaco.

AGATA: It's fitted so beautiful. And you're petite.

FIVE: It's so hard for me.

AGATA: You did a great job. Look at me, I'll fold it. You tell me when to stop.

(SIX *enters.*)

SIX: Can I come in fifteen minutes?

AGATA: I have a woman here, and I close at 4, so better to come tomorrow.

(SIX *exits.*)

AGATA: Let's see, can you button? Now face to the mirror. One sleeve. This one, visible longer. I'll explain you. Some people have different shoulders. Shoulders make one arm longer. Hip connection different. Just visual. Something big difference.

FIVE: Can you make them even?

AGATA: Yes. Some of the leather at the bottom of sleeve, you will lose.

FIVE: I had a trenchcoat and sent it to Burberry and they said sometimes it's better to cut from the shoulder.

AGATA: I don't cut from shoulder. Can you face to the mirror? Over shoulder, here cap. Cap wider. Here not enough fabric. It's complicated. I don't do that. *(Pinning)* Today everyone comes with fancy coat. One layer coat or double layer. I wouldn't be able to make that buttonhole. You care about buttonholes?

FIVE: Um.

AGATA: One place in the city makes buttonhole. They have machine. In garment district. It cost a lot of money. Twenty dollars for one buttonhole.

FIVE: That much?

AGATA: Yes, buttonholes like creating a picture. Piece of art. A lots of practicing need to know exactly. There and then they look beautiful which more better than commercial machine. No one wants to know how to make buttonhole. Same like shorten men shirts. Have to have intuition about how to do on sleeves. As more you do, build creativity. It's hard, it takes so long time. Time, time, and time and time. I don't have.

FIVE: *(Indifferent)* I didn't realize it was such a specialty.

AGATA: Very interesting. If we make a little longer we can keep one button. Also distance proportional.

FIVE: I'll never button that, so whatever.

AGATA: Change it please.

(FIVE *parts the fitting room curtain to reveal* VLAD *perched on a stool, a vision from twelve years ago, not a hair out of place, looking perfect in an impeccable snakeskin coat.*)

(*Bloomingdale's elevator music bops through the space.*)

VLAD: I hear you planning to leave Bloomingdale to become alteration lady.

AGATA: Who's this good-looking guy? Like a gangster. Look good, do bad things.

VLAD: You don't know at night, I have a secret alteration shop. Underground, at night. At night when you sleep.

AGATA: What you do at night?

VLAD: Can attach buttons all over places.

AGATA: Vlad, you very much liar.

VLAD: Everyone liar. That's why I'm member of Google Plus Society of Animal Lovers. When sun goes down. Animals own life. Every creature come closer to the edge. They feel safe to do whatever they want. The Black Sea. Big flat fish has extension on end, has electrical power can kill person.

AGATA: And how many snakes you need to kill to make your coat?

VLAD: In nature will survive who is toughest.

AGATA: Just to have some fashion.

VLAD: Bloomingdale make coat, not me. Coat hanging there.

AGATA: Snakes dangerous if you want to go closer to them. Some animals, that how it is.

VLAD: Some snakes can be very sweet. Make a little roll. Sleep on couch. Put head on knee.

AGATA: I never saw those snakes.

VLAD: My country, I went to zoo. They have sex with each other. I was very stressed and impressed. Every two minutes.

AGATA: Whole humanity are the same. Most children come not because women want children, because men want sex.

(Pause)

VLAD: You can be very powerful, Agata. People melting under your look.

AGATA: If you melting, take off your coat.

VLAD: I keep this coat in closet in plastic. Only wear for special occasion. Like first date. *(Pause)* I tell you straight to face. When I see you, my head goes dizzy. Tongue becomes white paper.

AGATA: Could be side effects. Your medication improve one side. Many more sides worse.

VLAD: It's side effects of you. Every woman are gold digger and can't do anything in bed. I know you different. I'm jealous on you. Especial your independency. Way how you can manage your life. *(Pause)* Agata, will you go out with me? *(Pause)*

Don't think too much. Not rock science.

AGATA: I'm not good at this. I think.

(VLAD offers his hand. She takes it. They take a few steps together, a duet of interconnectedness.)

VLAD: Let's go. *(He slips off into the darkness.)*

Scene 5

(JANICE *enters, shattering the reverie.*)

AGATA: Woman brought this green fabric. She want two decorative pillowcases. She say, "My husband, he doesn't shave. He contact fabric, it get destroyed because of face. This will be okay?"

JANICE: How would you know?

AGATA: Exactly. I say, "I really don't know." That was the highlight of the moment. She became really upset on me. "What, you know. You know many things." Yes, I'm tailor. I know how to make stitches. You know what? I do them *very* well. Give me size, I'll stitch it. I said, "Look, I'm not expert on husband's cheeks react against fabric."

(JANICE *laughs.*)

AGATA: Thank you for laughing. She didn't. She was so offended on me. Maybe I stop to care about many things. Whatever I think I can say daytime. When you're truthful you don't need to think later. Don't need to think before, middle, after. *Once.*

JANICE: What are we doing for her pillowcases?

AGATA: She wanted pillow, twenty-one and three quarters. She say, "What if do twenty-two? What would that give us?" I say, "Nothing. A quarter inch more." Her eyes became so unusual fascinated with this quarter. "Doesn't this make any difference, visual?" No. It's easier for me, twenty-two, that it.

JANICE: She's nuts. I used to have a client like her in a wheelchair. With all these fantasies about what I could do. She wanted a full tour of the city every time we went out. "You're healthy. Keep going." I was like, I can push you to the corner. "No, I wanna see what's around the corner." Okay, do you know how hard it is to cross the street? You have to raise it, and a thing comes down. It's a physical thing. I know how the chair works. It's just heavy. I understand, it's annoying to sit and see one thing all day, but I'm not Tarzan. I don't have that much strength to push through all the bumps on the road. I fall apart very easily.

AGATA: Live your life. You think you know many things. No, many things you don't know. You just know something.

JANICE: I finished these pants. (*She takes a pair of blue military pants out of a bag. A bright red stripe runs down the side.*)

AGATA: I'm glad you finished the sniper man's pants. He has a parade tomorrow.

JANICE: You know why they have the red stripe?

AGATA: The flag colors.

JANICE: No. It symbolizes blood. Eddie told me.

AGATA: Snipers are special people. He came ask me alter some jacket. On jacket was button big. Said "sniper with honor." After that I lost complete interest in sniper.

JANICE: Why?

AGATA: How do you get honor as a sniper? You kill someone. Sniper sitting there, waiting there person to pass, just kill them. Must kill people very well. Maybe he likes to killing. Go and fight with lions if you're that tough. (*Examining pants*) How much did you let them out? Three quarters or half inch?

JANICE: The ticket said three quarters. Look, the stitches are invisible like yours.

AGATA: Beautiful. You didn't see sniper man did you? (*Getting her phone*) He sent me picture in parade. What I did? Shorten pants only. Do I need to see you? No. Why do I need to see your shortened pants? He likes to have compliment. To sniper man I said, "You look handsome. We're all proud of you."

(JANICE *looks at the photo.*)

JANICE: I have a picture to show you, too. (*Getting her phone*) That's me and Eddie.

AGATA: (*Looking*) Oh, very nice.

JANICE: Right after he proposed. (*She dances in place.*)

AGATA: He propose you at the Staten Island Ferry boat?

JANICE: Yes, it was so romantic by the water.

AGATA: You don't have ring.

JANICE: It's being sized. It was his Grandma's. He just couldn't wait. (*Pause*) But he showed it to me. It's perfect. An antique. I hate modern engagement rings. You look like a Jello-mold dessert.

AGATA: Only a few month dating. Seems kind of all of a suddenly.

JANICE: I've known him my whole life. And we're getting old.

AGATA: You're babies. What your mom thinks?

JANICE: He won her over when he fixed the dryer. It's a gas dryer. So we were afraid the house would explode if we tried to pull it out from the wall. He did it like it was nothing. Didn't even use a dolly to roll it out. Just picked it up, well off the ground, with his bare hands. But like as big and tough as he is, he also keeps a purse with Chapstick and coins. He has both sides.

AGATA: (*Looking closer at a photo*) His pants.

JANICE: I know.

AGATA: One leg is longer.

JANICE: Yeah, I told him. He doesn't care.

AGATA: That bad sign.

JANICE: How?

AGATA: If you're ignorant on pants, you'll be ignorant on wife.

JANICE: I'll tell him you said that.

AGATA: Why you wanna take care of this loser?

JANICE: *(Amused)* Jeez.

AGATA: He will not be my husband. Really. In picture, *one leg longer*? Say him, "If you're gonna look like a poly roly, you better dress properly. Go with me, I like you to wear professional, not what you like. Or wear professional, or not be my husband."

JANICE: Okay *his pants aside* he's like a magical person to me. I don't know how to explain it.

AGATA: This man confused you.

JANICE: It's like all my needs and desires are met before I even ask. Like I was cracking eggs for our omelet this morning and a tiny piece of shell got into the egg white. You know how hard it is to get that out? You stick in a spoon and it just. Like it looks like you have it, the spoon is right under it, then as you lift up the spoon, it just slides right off the edge. But today without thinking I just went for it with my finger. I looked in the bowl and it was gone. I thought, impossible. I looked at my finger, and there it was. Stuck to my nail. My fingernail attracted the eggshell with some kind of a magnetic force or something.

AGATA: What this has to do with Eddie?

JANICE: That's never happened before. That's how I feel since I've been with him. About everything. I can trust stuff. Like the way the world works. You know? Like how we got together. It was meant to be. We want the same things.

AGATA: What things?

JANICE: We both want three kids.

AGATA: Mmm.

JANICE: What does "mmm" mean?

AGATA: I was planning to have three children. Looking back I think good idea I had one.

JANICE: I know it's expensive.

AGATA: Not just buy food. Raise child, you have to talk. Read books. So much time-taking care, you forget about yourself. Anything I did for her, I did for my pleasure. I don't feel punishment for decision having her. But three kids is a lot.

JANICE: He's gonna be a stay-at-home dad. We're gonna buy a house upstate.

AGATA: Upstate?

JANICE: We're just looking right now. We don't know if we can afford it.

AGATA: Three kids, you both need working.

JANICE: You paid off your mortgage by yourself working here.

AGATA: I did, yes. I bought apartment, 57. In Rego Park. I paid mortgage six and a half years not thirty years.

JANICE: Well, I'm gonna get my certificate and be like you.

(Pause)

AGATA: That mean you wanna take over?

JANICE: If your offer still stands, I think I could do it. I have a confidence that I didn't have before. Like now that I have Eddie, I can get in the flow more. It's like a spiritual thing. Like when I did the sniper's pants. I was calm and focused for four hours.

AGATA: This pants took you four hours?

JANICE: Yes. I wasn't bored. I wasn't fidgety. I was one with the pants.

AGATA: All you did was let out three quarter inch right?

JANICE: Yeah. Was I supposed to do something else?

AGATA: No. Honey, you need to practice more. You can't dance before you can't walk.

JANICE: I know. I can get better. That's the whole thing. I believe in myself now.

AGATA: But how could you do if upstate?

JANICE: Not that far up. Eddie's looking for places on the Metro- North line. They're probably more expensive, so it depends. I mean if it were up to me, we'd be looking for places in Queens, but I'm part of a couple now.

AGATA: Well, if you want to be making money, you should be working here. Good, honest, decent money. People who come here know: I go there, a woman will do it. Starting from scratch will be different. Can take years to build customers. People from the day first I open till this time still come to me. And more every day. It's quiet. Peaceful. You turn on your music.

JANICE: The more I think about it, the more excited I get.

AGATA: It is exciting, yes. You have to think deeper and wider. You can build the business more.

JANICE: How?

AGATA: For example. I wanna do hats for a long time. Bras without wires. Lace, cotton. Like a woman. Not all molded stuff Victoria's Secret. Custom-made bra specific for that person. Will be like a heaven. Put boobs in, relaxed and nice. Women. We lost our beauty. More feminine 1920, 1940. Not feminine like hooker from 42nd Street. Neckline open up to belly button, as tight as possible, all things out. If it really doesn't look nice, it's ugly. Should be all the beauty underneath.

JANICE: You know how to make bras?

AGATA: Like I always saying my daughter: if you need to do something, say you can do it, and do it. And doesn't have to be just you. Bring people outside US. Colombian good sewers. Brazil. Also from India. Could be also China. Could be invite people to make interviews. Through immigration department. Be sponsor, green card. Smallest wage, on top offer health insurance. Invite them here, they're yours. Contract ten years. Treat them with respect. They give back to you good teamwork. So many people ask custom-made. Take very long time. You could bring someone to do. Number two: Bridal addition. Many girls want to be a wife. Alteration wedding dresses very expensive. Then stylist for brides. So many, many, many ways. Whole building. You graduated business. You can organize management. Number three: You can take different place, small place, fitting place, Manhattan. Manhattan richer, can afford more pieces expensive, alteration higher. You can have styling agency. Stylist do shopping for people. Work celebrities. Hire stylist, one, two, three, four people. If I were forty-five years, I could do that. But now I'm exhausted.

(JANICE *stands up.*)

JANICE: (*Losing her balance*) Whoa.

(JANICE *starts hyperventilating.*)

AGATA: What wrong?

JANICE: (*Shallow breaths*) I stood up too quick. I get dizzy.

AGATA: Sit.

(JANICE *sits.*)

JANICE: *(Shallow breaths)* I'm fine. I just can't breathe.

AGATA: Should we go Urgent Care? They have new one on 30th.

JANICE: *(Shallow breaths)* No. I don't need. Another doctor. To tell me. I'm having a panic attack. It's embarrassing enough.

(AGATA *throws a garment in front of her.*)

AGATA: Here, I patched the other, you patch this. Keep cuff the same width, but shorter. Here's my needle. Go.

JANICE: *(Shallow breaths)* I can't.

AGATA: This good to do when you have problem. Work so you can breathe.

JANICE: *(Shallow breaths)* I don't know what happened. Sometimes I just spin out.

AGATA: Do you meditate?

JANICE: *(Shallow breaths)* I don't mess with pills.

AGATA: No. Meditate. That stage when you not thinking. Beautiful views in mind.

JANICE: *(Shallow breaths)* Oh. No.

AGATA: Best time of my day. After that you feel so clean. You energized your mind. Things happen different. Not you care less. You accept things. You should meditate, Janice. This work like meditating, too.

(JANICE's *breathing continues out of control. She is exposed here in a way that makes her desperately uncomfortable.*)

AGATA: Relax! Start to breathe. Inhale. Exhale through mouth. Start to do.

(JANICE *attempts labored, deep breaths.*)

JANICE: This is like. Do you ever when you're trying to sneeze, look at the light?

AGATA: Keep breathing.

(JANICE *picks up the needle and begins to stitch.*)

AGATA: Feel like under your skin something running. Physically, you can feel top of head through whole body, something smooth goes. You take iron wanna see smoothness, that what you feel. *(Pause)* Best place to meditate actually is in a steamer. Do you know steamer? On top a big, big rock. Put water and steam comes. Beat you with special branches in birch. Spring time new leaves come. Dry them until time to go to steamer. Put them in boiling water become fluffy again. Beat you and massage you. Not only all of a suddenly—have to know how to beat you, splash you with water. Very, very healthy. You know who liked that? Putin. He's a pure Russian. He wants everything in a bath.

JANICE: I don't think we have anything like that here. *(She continues stitching.)*

AGATA: Closest here is saunas at the gym. Just hot, hot steam. Sit ten minutes. As soon as feel hot, take cool shower. Vessels going wider and shrinking, bad stuff comes out. Tell you the truth. Sometimes I sleep in the sauna. Put towel down, lay down go to sleep. Pick time no one inside. Go to first bench. I lay there.

JANICE: I'll see if Eddie's gym has a sauna.

(JANICE *has settled into a calmer rhythm.*)

AGATA: Once you have the stitch, keep the rhythm. Inhale through nose, exhale through mouth. Ten, twelve times. Many years ago, I did this. When big problem with immigration I can't solve. That moment only me and me, no one else. Heard voice. In head. Pure Russian language. "Everything will be fine." Close eyes. I feel some tunnel with stars maybe black. My vision goes through, just stops somewhere. *(Pause)* Try to visualize some field. Positive wibes. Whatever you feel beautiful.

JANICE: (*Closing her eyes*) Yeah.

AGATA: You see something?

JANICE: (*Enraptured*) When Eddie lifted the dryer. His forearms tensed into these amazing lines like a harp or something. Uhhhh a heavenly stringed instrument that's just a natural part of him.

AGATA: Okay. Later on, more professional, take stairs go down and down and down, and at the bottom you'll see something more incredible interesting. Just don't be scared.

Scene 6

(*The curtains of the shop are drawn.* AGATA *works alone. Outside the shop, flip flops come into view just below the curtain.*)

(*There is a pound on the glass door.* AGATA *looks up.*)

VLAD: Agata, are you there?

(AGATA *doesn't move.*)

VLAD: Agata, I need to talk to you. I know you're there. (*He pounds on the glass.*) Agata!

AGATA: Why don't you open the lock like you say you can?

VLAD: I told you that for your safety. I would never do that.

AGATA: Oh, you told me you knock a woman down in 30 seconds for my safety, too?

(*Pause*)

VLAD: Actual, yes.

AGATA: I take care of my own safety.

VLAD: Please let me in. I just wanna talk to you.

AGATA: I have nothing to say you.

VLAD: Just listen. Please. Please forgive me. *(He pauses.)*

AGATA: Vlad, what will I say? I will not forgive you? I will forgive you? Just leave me alone. Go home.

VLAD: Please let me see you.

AGATA: I'm closed. *(She runs her machine.)*

VLAD: Agata, please! *(Pause)* Agata, I'm warning you!

(AGATA turns up music loud enough to drown out VLAD. A few moments pass. The pounding subsides. His flip flops walk off. She lowers her music. It is quiet. Until footsteps approach. The boots of two uniformed POLICE officers come into view.)

POLICEMAN: Ms Priechev? *(Knocking on the glass)*

(AGATA turns off her music.)

AGATA: Yes?

POLICEMAN: Ms Priechev, would you open the door?

(AGATA gets up and opens the door. POLICEMAN, POLICEWOMAN and VLAD filter in.)

POLICEMAN: Ms Priechev, this man is claiming you're holding his pants hostage.

AGATA: Ha! What type of hostage?

POLICEWOMAN: He's claiming he gave you a pair of pants to take in, and you never returned them.

AGATA: Where is the ticket?

(VLAD produces a ticket. The POLICE examine it, and hand it to AGATA.)

AGATA: This ticket is a lie. I never wrote it.

POLICEWOMAN: Do you have any other receipts we could see?

(AGATA hands them a spike of receipts.)

POLICEMAN: The handwriting does seem to match.

AGATA: I don't know how he got this ticket and copied my handwriting, but I didn't write this.

VLAD: Where are my white pants?

AGATA: You never gave me any pants. Stop this, Vlad.

VLAD: It's right here on the ticket. I was supposed to pick up today.

AGATA: Why do you think I keep your man's pants? I can't even wear it.

VLAD: You can sell it.

AGATA: What type of business I provide? Take customers' clothes and sell it? You know I never took your pants.

VLAD: You think you get away these things, you won't.

AGATA: Tell me how much pants cost, I'll pay you to go away.

VLAD: You see, she wants to pay me. That means she sells it at a higher price.

AGATA: Oh, you give me so big stress here! I try to explain you to leave me alone! I agree give you money so you leave me alone!

VLAD: Maybe she plans to return to store, get money that way.

POLICEMAN: Where'd you buy the pants, sir?

VLAD: Online.

POLICEMAN: How could she return them?

(*Pause*)

VLAD: She didn't know I buy online. Maybe she would try to take to a store.

POLICEWOMAN: How many years have you had this business, ma'am?

AGATA: Twelve years.

POLICEWOMAN: You think she could have a successful business for twelve years, if she took her customers' clothes and resold them?

VLAD: She tricks people!

POLICEWOMAN: Maybe your pants are at home. Check your closet.

VLAD: No, I know! She stole my pants! She must be held responsible!

(Pause)

POLICEMAN: Wanna go to court?

VLAD: They were my only white pants. Very unusual pants from Venezuela. They cannot be replaced.

POLICEWOMAN: Take it up with Judge Judy.

AGATA: *(To* VLAD*)* Yes, maybe I make a law case against you.

POLICEMAN: *(To* VLAD*)* Time to go, Bud.

AGATA: Take him away! Put the handicuffs on!

(The POLICE *escort* VLAD *out of the shop.)*

POLICEMAN: Sorry, to disturb you, ma'am.

AGATA: Think logical, Vlad. Not this cheap trick. A lie one hundred percent. Like when say Putin is so stupid to put his own bomb in Moscow apartments. Putin seven or eight times the smartest man. Bomb was military, not his job. See the politic behind. *(She struggles to settle back into work.)* I don't idolize anybody. But Putin likes his motherland. Outside enemy comes, you don't give up. Do everything to protect. Before everything was Russian Empire. Latvia, Moldavia, Poland, Lithuania, Estonia, Finland. Other fifteen republics. Gave freedom to people to become separate people. So people can't live in peace.

Newspapers not helping. Take one word. Twist it a hundred times. US like star on skies. Bad things, Putin. People don't like politics of Soviet Union. I know which part they don't like. Nobody likes that part. I wouldn't say Stalin was good man, he was evil man, but he was for country. He was power. Russian have bad side. But good side of Russians could die for motherland. Very strong, brave. Can fight until the last. Even if not possible to win. If people so strong inside, you have to kill them completely. Turkmenistan. Bord of Afghanistan. Southeast Soviet Union. If I wouldn't be born there, I wouldn't be so tough.

Scene 7

(JANICE *enters through the glass door with a large, black gift bag.*)

JANICE: Happy Mother's Day!

AGATA: Oh, thank you! The heart shape is kind of my enemy shape, but this is very unusual, I like it.

JANICE: Hold on, what did you just say was unusual?

AGATA: That what you got me.

JANICE: But how did you know what it was?

AGATA: I just got a feeling.

JANICE: *(Holding up the opaque paper bag)* Is it see through?

AGATA: No. Sometimes I can guess.

(JANICE *unveils what is indeed a heart-shaped, vinelike plant.*)

AGATA: Oh, it beautiful.

JANICE: Wait. Are you psychic?

AGATA: No.

JANICE: Then how'd you know?

AGATA: I just know sometimes. My daughter give
me gifts and I know what inside. My daughter
disappointed. Gave me box, heavy. I say face cream for
night. She say, "How you know?"

JANICE: What am I thinking right now?

AGATA: I have no idea.

JANICE: Agata, you wanna talk about expanding the
business this could be like a whole side operation.

AGATA: Guessing gifts?

JANICE: Is that the only way it works?

AGATA: Other time. That was gift, too. I was on couch
thinking: what could be so big? Big, long. Did not
touch. I guessed: framed dog picture. I wrote it on a
piece of paper. My daughter was upset again. *(Pause)*
Most important part when I guessed. Appointment
visa. Before night something came to mind—my
daughter shouldn't go. I say, "If you go, you'll lose
everything. Find different agency. More that you can
rely." I had a dream she already came. I kiss her on
her cheek. I feel like I kissed yesterday. This touch.
I knew she'll come. Daughter came here seventeen
year old. No papers. Need some income. Worked in a
sweatshop. They fired her. Then she got employment
card. And got everything proper way in London. That
where she lives now. Paid her completely tuition.
Got job with bank. Lives half million apartment in
London. When she goes outside on her balcony she can
see rainbows. To have apartment like this. Self-made
person. She has a good sample: me.

JANICE: So you've been able to read minds your whole
life?

AGATA: Not minds. First time, teapot. When was very
young somehow came to mind I'd break this teapot. My

mom said, "Look, if break it, I know not on purpose."
I broke it in front of her face. I wore robe in fashion
Japanese kimono. I pass, catch sleeve with teapot little
nose. It broke like this. I start to cry. Not because I
broke. Because I knew I was gonna break. I didn't know
how. I didn't wanna break. The stupid thing of the
teapot.

JANICE: You could charge people like an extra ten
dollars to tell them how their job interview is gonna go.
Or if they'll meet someone at the wedding. Or—

AGATA: No, then people kick me away because I'm
witch.

JANICE: People like psychics! They're very popular on
Long Island.

AGATA: I don't want to predict things, just comes to me.
Hard when you predict. Then things happen. You feel
uneven. Like the plane with bad weather. I don't think
those people who predict have easy life.

JANICE: I have a question for you—

AGATA: I have to take this plant home. There's a woman
in the neighborhood with a bad eye. She looks at the
plant, two days later it's dead.

JANICE: Is Eddie enough for me?

AGATA: What you mean enough?

JANICE: Like when we spend the whole day in bed, I
look at my phone and it's four o'clock and I panic like,
"You never got out of bed all day!" I wonder if I'm
wasting my time.

AGATA: I wonder the same.

JANICE: I build guys up in my head. I don't know if it's
real.

AGATA: I don't think he would buy house with you if not
serious.

JANICE: That's not happening now.

AGATA: Why not?

JANICE: He's in debt.

AGATA: Money's a problem for him.

JANICE: Money's not a problem for him. He doesn't have any.

AGATA: What does he do?

JANICE: He lives in fear of that question.

AGATA: Why?

JANICE: He basically does like semi-industrial amounts of laundry from re-selling thrift store stuff.

AGATA: So to make story short: he's not working.

JANICE: He's looking for something better. In the meantime, I'm just gonna move into his studio on Staten Island.

AGATA: You could come here every day from Staten Island?

JANICE: Maybe not everyday. It's three hours one way.

AGATA: Summer is busy, clients waiting outside all hour. Look in window. I don't have room enough invite people. Want me to go faster, I can't. Without me here, you have to be every day.

JANICE: I don't know.

AGATA: Janice, this is once and forever. I need to know what you gonna do. I don't want to stress your breathing, but I need to speak you straight and open. The rent going up next year and it was extra much before that. Since I paid my mortgage, I will not suffer from any complicated thing. In three month my lease is up, I have to decide what to do with this place.

JANICE: You mean if I don't take over, you won't renew the lease?

AGATA: Why should I work so hard? Better I should be out.

JANICE: Don't say that. God!

AGATA: Janice, stay down. Sit cool.

JANICE: It's not right, Agata. It's like the elephant in the corner. You know it, but you won't say it: your business is too important. You can't just give up on it. It's your life.

AGATA: Well.

JANICE: I have to talk to Eddie. Maybe we can figure something out.

AGATA: Janice, you do what best for you. Don't worry about my shop.

JANICE: No, you're offering me a huge opportunity. Your daughter flaked out and became a banker in London. I'm the only one who can keep your legacy going. You have no idea how much that means to me. My mom thinks I'm running my life down the drain. You have this kind of faith in me. That's a big deal. I promise I won't let you down.

Scene 8

(AGATA *is alone.*)

AGATA: Today gentleman, he gave me so big stress. That guy, he's a priest. Trinity Church Peter. Whoever priest I have, they're always like that. Never good to me. Like I'm outside, sitting, begging, treat you this way. (*Pause*) I let out a few people. If someone doesn't trust me, I let them out. For special people, I'm extra careful. But priests lie. Always: do for today, someone dying some place. Ask to do fast. Respect his profession. Whoever come for funeral, I'd leave everything for them. I'm not even religious. "Can you make pants short for *tomorrow*?" Have to go to someone die in hospital for confession. I do, and he doesn't come. Three or four months, I call him. "Oh, I forgot." Man is dead, or confession never happened. One bad person can spoil everything.

(VLAD *appears outside the glass window, almost unrecognizable, except for his flip-flops, wearing only undergarments. He enters the shop, disoriented.*)

AGATA: Vlad, sit down.

(VLAD *sits and may start to cry.*)

AGATA: Does your father know where you are?

(VLAD *doesn't respond.*)

AGATA: Should I call to your father?

VLAD: No!

AGATA: Did they let you out of hospital, or you ran away?

VLAD: They let me out.

AGATA: Where are your clothes?

VLAD: At my apartment.

AGATA: I'm calling to your father.

VLAD: No, my father is trying to kill me. I'm kicking him out.

AGATA: Vlad, your father is elderly man, ninety-two. He can't kill you. Shouldn't you stay more in hospital rather than come home and kick your father?

VLAD: You never support me!

AGATA: Vlad, I always support you. I came for Christmas. I baked pancake for you.

VLAD: But you left.

AGATA: Why did I leave, Vlad?

VLAD: I don't know!

AGATA: In Christmas you were putting things in box. I start to put things. Not the right way. You said, "Why put things like that?" I start to fix, turn this way, you took plastic and scratched my hand.

VLAD: That was by accident.

AGATA: No you stood there, you checked to see how I react.

VLAD: I didn't mean to scratch you!

AGATA: No, you meant, Vlad. This was the last thing you did to me.

VLAD: People in the world forgive Hitler and you can't forgive me?

(SIX *enters.*)

AGATA: Vlad, go to the fitting room, change it, please.

(VLAD *goes behind the curtain.* SIX *holds up a hoodie.*)

SIX: I need the zipper replaced.

AGATA: I don't do zippers.

SIX: Huh?

AGATA: The zipper, all of them different colorwise. Manhattan, spend half a day to get zipper. Customer: I don't like zipper.

SIX: No prob. I got one right here.

(SIX *presents* AGATA *with a zipper.*)

AGATA: Listen, zippers are very, very time-taking thing. Time- taking, stressful. If I spend so much time doing zippers, who will pay my rent?

SIX: It's a zipper. How hard can it be?

AGATA: I was very curious too, is there some trick I don't know? Checking right and left to see and learn. I sat two hours whole video. I did same, and I had miserable time. Need to have crazy experience, tough experience to do fast. I'm sorry, I can't do your zipper. Now I need to finish with this man. Goodbye, please.

(Six exits.)

AGATA: Vlad, you need to leave now. I can't have customers seeing you here. You smell.

(VLAD emerges from behind the fitting room curtain and goes straight for the door. Instead of leaving, he turns the key that was already in the lock and pulls out the set of keys, tucking them behind his back.)

AGATA: Unlock the door.

VLAD: Come home with me.

AGATA: No, I am here making living needle and thread! Your closet every coat Prada, Dolce and Gabbana. Your car sports Mercedes, I take subway wagon. You don't need to make living, I do!

VLAD: I need you, Agata.

AGATA: Give me the keys!

(VLAD evades AGATA.)

VLAD: Please, come home with me! Agata, please. They gave me twelve electric shots to my brain. They tried to delete my memory. I can't even turn on my computer. I don't remember how it works. I don't remember my password. I'm shamed to ask anyone else. Please.

(Pause)

AGATA: I can write it down for you.

VLAD: No. It won't make sense. You have very good patient. You help me understand.

AGATA: I can write the steps down. And your password. It's very simple.

VLAD: No, you have to come with me!

AGATA: I'm not going anywhere with you, Vlad.

(VLAD *picks up a chair and throws it at* AGATA*'s head. She ducks and it hits the wall. She grabs her phone.*)

AGATA: Okay, I'm calling to the police now. That it.

VLAD: Agata.

AGATA: I'm calling to the police. (*Her hands are shaking. She's having a hard time working her phone.*)

(VLAD *fumbles with the keys, frantically inserting the wrong ones. He finally stabs the lock with the right one, opens the door, and exits.*)

Scene 9

(JANICE *enters the shop and sits at* AGATA*'s machine, the swaying ghosts above her. She sighs and begins to look for something. Her phone chimes. She takes it out, and grins at the screen.*)

JANICE: Eddie just put a heart on my comment. I explained something too long and ended with, "I'm done now." And he made sure I knew he liked it. (*She puts a gown into a bag.*) That keeps happening. I think I have something to be embarrassed about, and he's so sweet and accepting. Even the first time he kissed me. I was way too shy. I kept walking away from him. He just hooked arms with me. And held my hands so tight. Like a vice grip. I thought, "Finally, I'm with a *real* man." (*Pause*) We were standing in front of my mom's house. Looking up the street for a cab that stopped at the wrong place. It was a foggy, warm night and droplets of mist were twirling in the headlights. Everything was suspended. I had this vision.

(Headlights cut through the shop, cocooning JANICE *in a haze. She picks up the bag and heads toward the door, looking out to see who might be coming. She waits.)*

JANICE: I was walking across a green meadow. Not sure which direction or how long it'll take. I see myself. Doing a backbend. And I have the idea to twirl around in the backbend position. So my hands make complicated crossover moves in the mud. Eddie senses I need him. He comes over and spots me. I can spring around light and quick. And we make beautiful designs together. I look up at his head with the mist behind him, and he's gorgeous. He has these plumes of high beams coming out like hair extensions.

(No one comes. JANICE *drops the bag on a chair.)*

JANICE: It was just that feeling of oh! This is what it is. This is what eternity feels like. An eternal bond, this is why people are together.

(The headlights flash off.)

Scene 10

(A Russian folk song plays. AGATA *emerges from behind the fitting room curtain to join* JANICE *in the shop.)*

AGATA: *(Turning down the volume on her phone)* I wanna stop this guy or make a little less.

JANICE: You don't have to. What is it?

AGATA: This song is in the heart of every tailor. State of mind. When fit on you well, you feel different. When client happy, you feel double pleasure.

JANICE: What's it called?

AGATA: Title of song. Starii Pidgak. Old Jacket. When he try his jacket in the end, tailor thought I'd be so happy, maybe I believe in love again. Tragic, but still hope. From first time I heard, I thought it was about me.

JANICE: That's interesting. *(Self-critical)* I should stop saying "that's interesting" because it means nothing. I just said nothing.

AGATA: *(Picking up a bag)* That woman supposed to come twenty-fifth, she didn't.

JANICE: I was here till eight-thirty.

AGATA: Thank you for sitting special. I was in emergency.

JANICE: Oh, I was glad I could help!

AGATA: Some people yelling, putting very bad review on internet. I said, I have person sit there from seven to eight o'clock on the twenty-fifth. You can come collect things. Be a little compassion. I didn't do for my pleasure, I have kidneys problem.

JANICE: Did the doctors figure out what was causing the swelling?

AGATA: Doctors say nothing helpful. Adrenaline not work like it supposed to be. You go to doctor, they don't give you any nice advices. Many people think get sick, doctor give them miracle pill. Doctor doesn't have anything what you need. They want you to be out of this world maybe.

JANICE: So I have some news.

AGATA: Eddie wanna get off Staten Island?

JANICE: Well. Yes. But that's not the news. I mean that's part of it. The news is. I'm expecting.

AGATA: Expecting what?

JANICE: Like to have a baby.

AGATA: Oh yes. Every bride expecting this.

JANICE: No, I mean now.

(Pause)

AGATA: You pregnant!

JANICE: Yes.

AGATA: Oh, Janice! Why you not say it, you pregnant?

JANICE: For some reason I can't bring myself to say that word.

AGATA: Why?

JANICE: I don't know. When I told my mom it was like a war broke.

AGATA: Why?

JANICE: We're not even married yet.

AGATA: So? Does the Bible say this no good thing? Americans pay too much attention to the Bible; five thousand before the C, after the C. New Bibles, Old Bibles. Who wrote the Bible? A bunch of drunk men to control women.

JANICE: I'm not familiar with that interpretation, but I like it.

AGATA: You pregnant is wonderful. Married or not. I believe that because I have no beliefs.

JANICE: She also says I'm not prepared. She's right about that.

AGATA: Even when you plan it as better as you can, it goes, goes, goes like roller coaster. That life.

JANICE: I was shocked when I found out. I was happy. But a scared kind of happy. Like maybe I was dumb to be so happy cause who knows what's coming. I could feel an attack coming on. Right when I started losing my breath, I closed my eyes and tried to visualize like you said. It helped.

AGATA: Did you see anything?

JANICE: Actually, yeah. The face of Eddie's six year old nephew just popped in my head. He told me he knew I was lonely. Because I liked owls and squirrels. Only the loneliest people like owls and squirrels.

AGATA: What this mean?

JANICE: I don't know but it got the job done. My mind stopped doubt- swirling. It just came to me: Move in with Eddie's parents.

AGATA: Where are they?

JANICE: Ohio.

AGATA: Wow.

JANICE: All his family moved out there. Four brothers. They all have kids already. We'll have a lot of support. *(Uncertain)* So that's good. *(Pause)* Are you disappointed in me?

AGATA: I'm not upset on you. I want you do whatever your heart feel to do. *(Pause)* I'm happy for you, Janice. You change dramatically when you become mama. In better way. Jaws drop.

JANICE: Did you?

AGATA: When my daughter born. Very proud having child. Two, three days after. Free from hospital. Passing street. Cars so fast. I have to be double careful. I have child. Nobody knows, but: I have a child. Very important for whole world. I was for her my whole life.

JANICE: That's sweet.

AGATA: She still gives me present, too, for her birthday. "Why did you give me?" She say, "All your suffering for child." It's true. Not only her. Something I did, too, that day. No pain killers. Nothing. I thought I'm dying. If I'm dying, that how it is, that okay. But I feel like loser. Other women did, I can't. I had appendix removed when five months pregnant. Spent all months in hospital until I give birth. Daughter five kilo; three kilo normal; five kilo is eleven pounds.

JANICE: Holy crap.

AGATA: The condition is type of: this child be alive and you die.

JANICE: That's terrifying.

AGATA: Don't be terrifying. Words and thoughts, material. Have energy special. If you think good things, they'll come.

(*Pause*)

JANICE: What about the shop?

AGATA: What about? My days are measured. The lease over soon.

JANICE: I can help you find someone else. There's a girl in my class better than me. A white blonde with dreadlocks.

AGATA: No.

JANICE: I can post signs at FIT. We can interview people.

AGATA: No, I thought I need someone I know here. Not someone I never seen one stitch made by their hands. (*Pause*) What I asked you not really fair, Janice. Not possible someone else do what I do. Even though altering, still creating something new. Most things I do just once. This kind of coat, first time, last time in life. One side fabric, other side leather. Customer comes in, immediately you have to know what to do, and put a price on it. Very something special. How to look attractive. I don't know why I know. Part of the art I have inside me. Something else inside. Something else I can feel there. Can't pass this. Can teach stitches and seams and skill. But more you can't pass. When I finish this place, be out of business plain. That how it should be.

(Pause)

JANICE: But what are you gonna do?

AGATA: I have so many things to do. I have to finish this complicated coat. First, I have to eat. Not hungry. Have to prepare for battle. *(She gets a handmade protein bar out of her purse.)* I got the recipe from Google Plus. Almond meal, hemps seeds, coconut flour, and dates have ability to stick things together, all proportions. Wanna try?

JANICE: *(Pause)* No, thanks. You know, Eddie said we could have people come to his parents' house. They're putting a sewing machine in the basement.

AGATA: Not many people come to home. Not like Starbuck your home. But if you planning to have home calls, have someone there if men call.

JANICE: Really?

AGATA: I don't wanna be bad predictor, but men unpredictable. Touch them, they feel different. Body can't control self. Many times I do my fitting. "Do you like it?" "Yes." Body part get excited, goes up. Body part works. Very much visible.

JANICE: I think I can focus on being a mom for a while. *(She exits.)*

Scene 11:
Parade of Customers

(The same parade of CUSTOMERS, now dressed in identical nursing scrubs, enters the shop, clearing all sewing paraphernalia. AGATA hands her work vest over to SEVEN.)

SEVEN: Hey, I wrote you a good review. Why did you delete it?

(AGATA may sit on a desk like it's a medical exam table.)

AGATA: I didn't. Yelp does this. They put you in garbage. They like to put in garbage.

(AGATA *may pull a hidden drawstring so that* SEVEN's *drab V-neck magically transforms into a cinched-in peplum top.* EIGHT *approaches* AGATA.)

EIGHT: Have you looked? You're down to one star.

(AGATA *may yank* EIGHT's *pantleg so that the scrubs instantly poof out into stylish wide-leg pants.*)

AGATA: Sorry, I don't have power over them. Not Yelp, not Google. That search agent puts wrong hours, wrong address. Put my phone number on restaurant in Soho. People called, order food.

SEVEN: *(Placing a stethoscope on her chest)* Can't you have that fixed?

AGATA: I tried to contact with Google. Google they are trillions people, never call back. People walking 36th Avenue in cold weather. Call me: "Where are you really located?" I can't change Google map, can you? Might take a whole year.

(SEVEN *and* EIGHT *exit. The cleared-out shop has taken on the sterile, institutional look of a hospital room.*)

AGATA: Good thing to get older. I have so big compassion to teenagers. Child is fourteen year, parents be thirty-four. What does thirty-four person know? Can't put two by two together. Live life very complicated not your fault.

(VLAD *enters in scrubs.*)

AGATA: I look on life path, I don't have any regret. The past is dead body in basement.

(VLAD *offers* AGATA *his hand. She doesn't take it.*)

AGATA: Chance to return back. I don't want to. Return back and live life? I don't even wanna be human. Not animal. A tree or something like that.

(VLAD *slips away with subtle movements echoing their earlier duet.*)

(*As he exits, eerie sounds of a hospital may begin may begin to seep in from the other side of the fitting room curtain.*)

(*Monotonous beeps and whirs blending with angelic tones.*)

AGATA: Now I feel so good, when I go to sleep, I can sleep in two minutes. I can sleep twelve hours. I just ashamed to sleep so much. I never wake up unless my cat bothers me.

(*A single, hanging garment falls to the floor.* AGATA *picks it up and puts it on. It's a flared, navy blue dress coat that fits her perfectly.*)

AGATA: Whenever he was eating, my grandfather, cat would come and eat food. He was so crying for cat when died. He had a heart attack. Don't know why. Maybe because old. Maybe cat. Maybe two both together.

(*Empty garments continue to fall in blurs of animal prints, pinstripes, satin, and denim.*)

(*Each one a flailing, biomorphic form, an image of rapid-fire release, shedding skin, letting go.*)

AGATA: I can't believe in this age as a human I appreciate life more than when I was younger. I feel absolutely good now. More free time to enjoy. European movies. White letters on a black screen. Slow. So you can read. No robots. No smash killings. I want to own those movies. I'll be looking at them forever.

(*The garment racks are bare rails, all of the fabric flaring in a glorious heap at* AGATA'*s feet. She almost appears to float.*)

(*The storefront glass door begins to glow. Reticent,* AGATA *adjusts her coat and takes a step toward the light.*)

(*Blackout*)

END OF PLAY